Inner Drive

52-Week Mental Health Journal for Men

Inner Drive

52-Week Mental Health Journal for Men

Build Focus, Resilience, and Daily Strength
with a Guided Journal for Self-Reflection,
Stress Relief, and Emotional Clarity

Aria Capri Publishing
Devon Abbruzzese
Mauricio Vasquez

Authors:
Aria Capri Publishing
Devon Abbruzzese
Mauricio Vasquez

First Printing: July 2025

ISBN - 978-1-998729-61-6 (Hardcover Book)
ISBN - 978-1-998729-60-9 (Paperback)

FREE BONUS

Enjoy a Free Digital Copy of This Transformational Journal—My Gift to You

Thank you for showing up for yourself and taking this powerful step toward daily self-care, reflection, and personal growth.

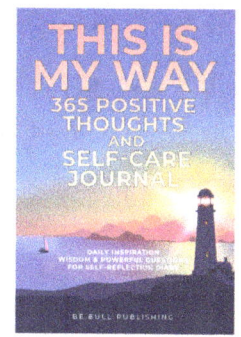

As a heartfelt gift, I'm offering you a FREE digital copy of THIS IS MY WAY: 365 Positive Thoughts and Self-Care Journal.

It's packed with inspiring messages and thought-provoking questions to help you build confidence, reduce anxiety, and reconnect with what matters most —all year long.

Claim your free e-copy by scanning this QR code:

Prefer a Physical Copy?

Many readers love having a physical copy to hold, highlight, or gift to someone special. If that sounds like you, you can grab your printed copy here:

Buy the hardcover version on Amazon by scanning this QR code:

Thank you for allowing me to be a small part of your self-care journey.

Here's to a year of reflection, growth, and positive change.

A Small Favor That Makes a Big Impact

If this journal has helped you pause, reflect, reconnect, or grow in even the smallest way—I'd be deeply grateful if you'd consider leaving a review.

As an independent author, I rely on the honest words of readers like you to help others discover this book. Your feedback not only supports the continued life of this work—it also reminds me why these quiet moments of reflection matter, one person and one page at a time.

You can share your thoughts by scanning the QR code. It only takes a minute, but your words have the power to help someone else begin their own journaling journey.

Thank you, truly, for being part of this. Your time, voice, and support mean more than you know.

Devon

Want More Journals and Resources?

Whether you're enjoying this journal and want to explore more titles, or you're looking for a digital version you can use on your device, you've got options!

 Print On Demand Store – Physical Copies

Use this QR code to visit our Amazon store and order printed editions of our books.

🪴 Gumroad Store – PDF Versions at a Lower Price

Scan this QR code to access our Gumroad store, where you can purchase downloadable PDF versions of our books at a lower price— perfect for printing at home or using digitally.

This journal belongs to

_____

Disclaimer

This journal is intended for personal reflection and general mental wellness support. It is not a substitute for professional advice, diagnosis, or treatment.

If you are experiencing emotional distress, a mental health crisis, or any situation that feels overwhelming, please seek guidance from a licensed physician, counselor, psychologist, or qualified mental health professional.

The author and publisher do not assume responsibility for any actions taken or not taken based on the content of this book. Use of this journal is entirely at the reader's discretion.

Your well-being matters—please reach out for professional help when needed.

Introduction

This journal isn't here to fix you. It's here to focus you.

Over the next 52 weeks, you'll be invited to take a few quiet minutes each day to check in—with your thoughts, your goals, and your mindset. The purpose isn't perfection. It's growth.

Consistency. Mental clarity. And stronger self-leadership in your everyday life.

You don't need to write like a poet or dig into deep emotions you're not ready to face. You just need to show up with honesty and take five to ten minutes for yourself—every day.

This journal gives you structure, guidance, and space to reflect in a way that's practical, personal, and forward-moving.

Each week revolves around a specific focus—rooted in four key areas that shape your mental well-being:

Calm and Resiliency, Connection and Engagement, Healthy Living, and Goals and Purpose.

Think of these as tools, not theories. Over time, you'll begin to recognize patterns in how you think, recover from stress, build relationships, and keep moving forward when life throws you off. That's where strength is built—from the inside out.

This journal is your space to track that growth. A place to gain control over your focus. And a tool to strengthen your emotional edge—day by day.

Calm and Resiliency

Everyone gets knocked down. What matters is how you get back up—and how long it takes to steady yourself. This section focuses on how you handle pressure, process stress, and regain mental clarity in the middle of everyday chaos.

You'll explore the habits that help you stay mentally sharp, control emotional noise, and keep your cool when things get turbulent. Calm doesn't mean being passive. It means keeping your center when everything else is spinning.

Resilience means building that center day by day—so you're ready for whatever's next. These prompts will help you develop habits that restore your calm under pressure and build a stronger internal baseline for your performance and peace of mind.

Connection and Engagement

You don't need to be surrounded by people to feel connected —but you do need the right ones. This section is about the relationships that keep you grounded and the quality of your interactions—with others and with yourself.

It's easy to go silent when you're dealing with pressure or burnout. But the truth is: meaningful relationships are a key part of resilience. The prompts in this section will help you reflect on the people who matter most, explore the kind of friend or partner you want to be, and consider how engagement—not isolation—helps sharpen your mental game.

Whether it's a mentor, a buddy, a partner, or your own inner voice, connection can be a fuel source. This is your chance to look at what strengthens those bonds and how to show up in them with more intention.

Healthy Living

Mental clarity starts with the basics: sleep, fuel, movement, and habits. You can't outrun stress or solve burnout without taking care of the physical foundations of your health. This section helps you check in on those basics—without guilt or pressure.

You'll reflect on what routines help you feel stronger. What slows you down. What habits are overdue for an upgrade. You'll track the small adjustments that sharpen your focus, steady your mood, and restore your drive.

You'll also explore the ways your mind benefits from fresh input—new learning, a shift in perspective, or a break from overstimulation. This is where performance and well-being intersect: in practical choices, built consistently.

Goals and Purpose

You don't have to be hustling all the time. But you do need something to aim for. Purpose doesn't have to be loud or dramatic. It just needs to matter—to you. This section helps you clarify what motivates you, what progress looks like for you, and how to move toward it with focus.

You'll examine what gets you stuck—and what pulls you forward. The prompts here encourage you to set your own pace, define your own version of success, and reconnect with goals that energize and challenge you.

Whether you're building something new or rebuilding after a setback, these questions help you keep your momentum. You'll reconnect with your drive—not just for what you want to accomplish, but for who you want to become along the way.

How to Use This Journal

Start on any day. Keep it where you'll see it—on your desk, in your gym bag, by your bed.

Write once a day, even if it's just a sentence. Some days the words will flow. Other days, not so much. Keep going. It's the habit that counts.

If you miss a day, don't quit. Just begin again. The goal isn't to be perfect—it's to stay in motion.

This journal is a quiet, private space. A reset button. A mirror. A tool you'll sharpen over time. You'll be surprised how much a few minutes of reflection can build your focus, improve your mood, and strengthen your mindset.

Calm and Resiliency

1. If your top three wishes were granted tomorrow, how would that change the way you show up in your life?

....

....

....

....

....

2. Which of your wishes are within reach through your own actions or decisions?

....

....

....

....

....

3. What simple activities lift your mood? How can you fit more of them into your week?

....

....

....

....

....

4. What strengths have helped you push through tough moments? How can you lean on them again?

....

....

....

....

....

5. What's a short phrase you can repeat to stay focused and centered under pressure?

....

....

....

....

....

6. What mental or physical practices build your ability to rebound from tough days?

....

....

....

....

....

7. How do you decompress after a long week? What helps you reset?

....

....

....

....

....

Connection and Engagement

1. What are some ways you stay in touch with people who matter to you?

....

....

....

....

....

2. Imagine your best friend wrote to encourage you—what would they say to lift your spirits?

....

....

....

....

....

3. Who brings clarity, humor, or insight into your life? What do you value about those exchanges?

....

....

....

....

....

4. Who have you lost touch with? What might make it easier to check in again?

....

....

....

....

....

5. When did you last unwind with a friend? What made that time feel good for you?

....

....

....

....

....

6. Think of two people you're grateful for. What words might you use to let them know they matter?

....

....

....

....

....

7. What everyday activities could you turn into shared moments with people you enjoy?

....

....

....

....

....

Healthy Living

1. What healthy changes would help you feel more focused, strong, or energized?

....

....

....

....

....

2. What tools, habits, or support might help you follow through on a change you care about?

....

....

....

....

....

3. How do you support your body's strength and recovery? What routines or habits feel helpful?

....

....

....

....

....

4. What are your current stressors? What actions have helped ease them, even a little?

....

....

....

....

....

5. Recall a high-stress moment—what signs showed up in your body or mood?

....

....

....

....

....

6. What stress relief strategies work best for you? How does your mind or body respond?

....

....

....

....

....

7. When you took a moment to check in with your body, what stood out? What shifted afterward?

....

....

....

....

....

Goals and Purpose

1. What would progress or growth look like for you by the end of this journal journey?

....

....

....

....

....

2. What's one clear step you could take to start making your goals a reality?

....

....

....

....

....

3. When you were younger, who or what did you imagine becoming? What influenced the path you've taken since then?

....

....

....

....

....

4. What internal or external roadblocks do you hit—and what keeps you moving forward anyway?

....

....

....

....

....

5. What type of work would bring out your best—if there were no limits holding you back?

....

....

....

....

....

6. If you could revisit the past or look ahead to the future, which would you choose—and why? What would you hope to learn?

....

....

....

....

....

7. What tool or habit might help you stay focused and on top of your plans this coming week?

....

....

....

....

....

Calm and Resiliency

1. What's one thing weighing on you today? Jot it down now—and revisit it when you feel clearer.

....

....

....

....

....

2. What one word could help you stay grounded today—and how might you put it into action?

....

....

....

....

....

3. After a deep breath, what do you notice in your body or focus? Has anything softened or shifted?

....

....

....

....

....

4. What strengths—physical and mental—give you confidence or pride?

....

....

....

....

....

5. What was a challenge you pushed through—and what did it show you about your resilience?

....

....

....

....

....

6. What's one simple way you could connect with someone today to feel more steady or supported?

....

....

....

....

....

7. What environment helps you decompress? What would it take to create that space at home?

....

....

....

....

....

Connection and Engagement

1. What group or social activity feels deeply satisfying afterward? What makes it so engaging?

....

....

....

....

....

2. Describe a time when someone really "got" you. What stuck with you about that moment?

....

....

....

....

....

3. Is there someone you've lost touch with lately? What's one low-key way to reconnect?

....

....

....

....

....

4. Describe a time when showing up led to an unexpected but valuable connection.

....

....

....

....

....

5. What compliment hit home for you—and why did it matter?

....

....

....

....

....

6. What are some stories with friends or family that still make you smile? What made them meaningful?

....

....

....

....

....

7. Who deserves a message of appreciation or reconnection from you? What would you say?

....

....

....

....

....

Healthy Living

1. What are your go-to ways of maintaining your well-being each week? How consistent are they?

....

....

....

....

....

2. How can you create a space at home that helps you unwind or recharge with ease?

....

....

....

....

....

3. What five actions would help you stay physically sharp and emotionally balanced?

....

....

....

....

....

4. What practice—even brief—could help you feel more grounded or content starting today?

....

....

....

....

....

5. When have you worried more than necessary? What did you learn about managing stress in hindsight?

....

....

....

....

....

6. What adjustments could make your home more energizing or restful for you?

....

....

....

....

....

7. What's your first step toward improving your environment—and why does it matter to you?

....

....

....

....

....

Goals and Purpose

1. What's one meaningful goal you haven't hit yet? What's held you back?

....

....

....

....

....

2. How could you create a simple action plan to move steadily toward your goal?

....

....

....

....

....

3. What's one ambition you've had professionally—and what's your first step toward it?

....

....

....

....

....

4. Where would you escape to for a short break—and what would you do to reset?

....

....

....

....

....

5. What milestones would your future self be proud of—and what message would you want to send him?

....

....

....

....

....

6. What are four things you enjoy but haven't done lately? How could you fit one into each weekend?

....

....

....

....

....

....

7. What's one change that could boost your focus and productivity next week?

....

....

....

....

....

....

Calm and Resiliency

1. What would an ideal start to your day look like—and what small step would get you closer to it?

....

....

....

....

....

2. What's on your go-to playlist—and how does each song shape your mood?

....

....

....

....

....

3. When were you last in a tough headspace—and what did that challenge teach you afterward?

....

....

....

....

....

4. What do you do when you need to clear your head and reset? How does it help?

....

....

....

....

....

5. Picture your favorite color filling the room. What shifts in how you feel?

....

....

....

....

....

6. Imagine being outdoors at sunrise—what do you hear, see, or feel in that calm moment?

....

....

....

....

....

7. What mental or physical tools do you lean on when life throws a curveball? What else might you try?

....

....

....

....

....

Connection and Engagement

1. Who would you bring together for a meaningful reunion—and what activities would help you reconnect?

....

....

....

....

....

2. Who brings out your best self? What traits in them leave a lasting impact on you?

....

....

....

....

....

3. Who's shaped your values, drive, or character? What lessons did they leave with you?

....

....

....

....

....

4. What's one small way you could look out for someone else— and what would that bring you in return?

....

....

....

....

....

5. What's on your "someday" list that would be better with a friend beside you? Who would you invite?

....

....

....

....

....

6. If you had extra time, money, or energy—who would you support? What difference would you want to make in their life?

....

....

....

....

....

7. What support or help could you offer someone close—and how would that reflect your values?

....

....

....

....

....

Healthy Living

1. What energizing meals or snacks do you enjoy most? Are they part of your regular routine?

....

....

....

....

....

2. How would you rate your current health habits? What's one small step that could improve them?

....

....

....

....

....

3. How do you decompress at the end of the day? Does it actually leave you feeling better?

....

....

....

....

....

4. When you think of your favorite spot, what do you feel physically or mentally?

....

....

....

....

....

5. What time of day do you feel sharpest or strongest—and how do you use that energy?

....

....

....

....

....

6. What beverages help you feel strong or sharp? Could they become part of your regular flow?

_____

_____

_____

_____

_____

7. When you're under pressure, what three things help you stay centered or come back to yourself?

_____

_____

_____

_____

_____

Goals and Purpose

1. What are your main goals and core needs for the week—and how can you plan to honor both?

....

....

....

....

....

2. What's driving you to keep showing up and pushing toward your aims these days?

....

....

....

....

....

3. What's your emotional response when a goal is delayed or missed? How do you handle that space?

....

....

....

....

....

4. What mental patterns or doubts tend to block your progress?

....

....

....

....

....

5. What mental shifts or actions can help you counter the doubts holding you back?

....

....

....

....

....

6. What three forces—people, values, or routines—help you push forward each day?

....

....

....

....

....

7. How do you personally define success—and how does that guide your decisions?

....

....

....

....

....

Calm and Resiliency

1. Which song helps you slow down or reset? What is it about?

....

....

....

....

....

2. What actions or mindsets help you recover when things don't go as planned?

....

....

....

....

....

3. What phrases would a trusted friend say to lift your spirits? Let yourself hear those words today.

....

....

....

....

....

4. Think back to a tough time you overcame—what showed you your own strength?

....

....

....

....

....

5. What's your ideal weather for feeling good or clear-headed? How do you like to spend time in it?

....

....

....

....

....

6. What childhood experience reminds you of fun, freedom, or connection?

....

....

....

....

....

7. Is there something in your space that reminds you of a meaningful time? What's the story behind it?

....

....

....

....

....

Connection and Engagement

1. What do you enjoy doing most with friends that helps you feel relaxed or recharged?

....

....

....

....

....

2. What meaningful interaction with a loved one do you still remember clearly from last year?

....

....

....

....

....

3. What strengths or traits in a friend or family member earn your respect or admiration?

....

....

....

....

....

4. Who's your go-to when things get tough? What's their style of support?

....

....

....

....

....

5. What solid advice from a trusted person made a difference in your thinking or action?

....

....

....

....

....

6. How would someone who knows you well describe your character, mindset, and energy?

....

....

....

....

....

7. Who showed you support or care this week—and how might you return that gesture?

....

....

....

....

....

Healthy Living

1. What movements or pauses help you stay sharp and loose at home or on the job?

....

....

....

....

....

2. How did standing tall and taking a breath shift your awareness or energy?

....

....

....

....

....

3. When did you last feel truly hydrated? What system could help you stay on track daily?

....

....

....

....

....

4. How's your recent sleep quality? Is there a simple change that could help you rest better?

....

....

....

....

....

5. What would an ideal evening routine look like to set you up for a strong start tomorrow?

....

....

....

....

....

6. Did a dream ever leave you with a surge of hope or clarity? Describe that moment.

....

....

....

....

....

7. What beverage helps you stay balanced, alert, or grounded? What's the impact?

....

....

....

....

....

Goals and Purpose

1. What's one straightforward goal you could focus on this week—and what would the benefit be?

....

....

....

....

....

2. What actions make you feel useful or fulfilled? What do they reflect about what drives you?

....

....

....

....

....

3. Describe a practical space you'd design to help you think clearly, plan well, and take action.

....

....

....

....

....

4. With unlimited financial freedom, how would your mission shift —or stay steady?

....

....

....

....

....

5. What single wish would remove a barrier or add meaning to your life? What difference would it make?

....

....

....

....

....

6. What three priorities will move you forward this week—and what's your plan to act on them?

....

....

....

....

....

7. What do you enjoy or value about your work or hobbies? What makes you stick with them?

....

....

....

....

....

Calm and Resiliency

1. Recall a moment from a specific age in your life. What stands out about that time?

....

....

....

....

....

2. Would you choose the beach or the mountains for a reset—and what does that say about your current state?

....

....

....

....

....

3. What past moment would you rewrite if given the chance—and what new path might it have opened?

....

....

....

....

....

4. Do sunny days or rainy ones help you reset better? Describe how that kind of day affects your mindset.

....

....

....

....

....

5. What music gets your energy up or helps you feel steady? What are your top ten feel-good tracks?

....

....

....

....

....

6. What's currently working in your life—even if it's small? How does recognizing it affect your perspective?

....

....

....

....

....

7. What five small activities could bring you ease or fun next week? Can you build them into your schedule?

....

....

....

....

....

Connection and Engagement

1. Who helps you feel alive, energized, or like yourself? What do they do differently?

....

....

....

....

....

2. What kind of event would best honor a close friend's personality or shared memories?

....

....

....

....

....

3. Who would you bring on a dream trip—and what strength or vibe would they add to the journey?

....

....

....

....

....

4. What kinds of conversations build trust or ease between you and others?

....

....

....

....

....

5. Where in your community do you feel connected or at ease around others?

....

....

....

....

....

6. Who would you enjoy hearing live—and how would the sound, energy, or crowd affect your mood?

....
....
....
....
....

7. What five traits stand out in a person you trust deeply? What do those traits mean to you?

....
....
....
....
....

Healthy Living

1. What did observing the sky bring up for you in terms of mindset, perspective, or calm?

....

....

....

....

....

2. What's your current self-image? How close is it to how you want to feel and show up?

....

....

....

....

....

3. Imagine being a pro athlete. What would your training and self-care need to look like to perform well?

....

....

....

....

....

4. When did you last move your body in nature? What shift did it create in your energy or headspace?

....

....

....

....

....

5. What's your current relationship with nutrition and fitness? What works—and what feels like a stretch?

....

....

....

....

....

6. How do you feel emotionally about food choices and habits? Is there room for a different approach?

....

....

....

....

....

7. Imagine a day where your choices reflect your health goals. What would that day include?

....

....

....

....

....

Goals and Purpose

1. What's one way you've helped someone feel better recently—or what held you back?

....

....

....

....

....

2. List 10 ways you can show up meaningfully for others. How do those acts reflect your values?

....

....

....

....

....

3. What legacy or impression do you want to be known for?

....

....

....

....

....

4. Would you pick physical vitality or financial abundance? What motivates your choice?

....

....

....

....

....

5. What practical wins this week would help you feel capable and steady?

....

....

....

....

....

6. What's a standout achievement in your life, and what strength did it require?

....

....

....

....

....

7. If you spent a day at a museum this weekend, who would you bring—and what would you want to check out together?

....

....

....

....

....

Calm and Resiliency

1. What sounds or actions bring you back to center when stress hits? How can you use them more regularly?

....

....

....

....

....

2. If you unplugged for 24 hours, what would you focus on—and how might that benefit you?

....

....

....

....

....

3. What came up in your mind during three minutes of silence? What do those thoughts tell you?

....

....

....

....

....

4. What action or habit helps you shake off stress and feel better?

....

....

....

....

....

5. Sitting by water—what do you notice with your senses, and how does it ground or calm you?

....

....

....

....

....

6. Today I feel solid about who I am because... (Complete the sentence.)

....

....

....

....

....

7. Describe a time you faced fear head-on. What did it teach you about courage or clarity?

....

....

....

....

....

Connection and Engagement

1. What group activities help you connect or unwind around others you know casually?

....

....

....

....

....

2. What kind of involvement in your community would reflect your strengths or values?

....

....

....

....

....

3. If you were side by side with a friend on a shoreline walk, what topics would you dive into?

....

....

....

....

....

4. Think back to your first close friend. What kinds of things did you do together?

....

....

....

....

....

5. What part of going to the theater sticks with you—sound, vibe, connection, or something else?

....

....

....

....

....

6. What light or fun memory from grade school still brings a smile?

....

....

....

....

....

7. If you could escape to a fantasy world, who'd be at your side—and what would your adventure look like?

....

....

....

....

....

Healthy Living

1. What language would you like to master—and how would you go about using it in real life?

....

....

....

....

....

2. What kind of series leaves you feeling good or relaxed—and why do you keep coming back to it?

....

....

....

....

....

3. Imagine a cruise anywhere. What would you do to recharge or explore along the way?

....

....

....

....

....

4. What phase of your life felt healthiest—and what routines or choices were in place?

....

....

....

....

....

5. What outfits boost your confidence or comfort—and why?

....

....

....

....

....

6. What subjects do you snap often—and what would you explore visually with better gear?

....

....

....

....

....

7. How do you recover or refuel when the week's been full?

....

....

....

....

....

Goals and Purpose

1. What three milestones would you want to tell your future self you've achieved?

....

....

....

....

....

2. What feelings surface when you remember a proud moment? What strength helped you get there?

....

....

....

....

....

3. What are you grateful for right now—and how does it keep you grounded?

....

....

....

....

....

4. If you landed on a new planet, what would you do or build there—and what would you want to feel?

....

....

....

....

....

5. If money wasn't a concern, what mission would fuel you—and who would be impacted?

....

....

....

....

....

6. Think of a teacher who shaped you—what would you write to honor that impact?

....

....

....

....

....

7. Where would your ideal job take you—and what kind of life would you build around it?

....

....

....

....

....

Calm and Resiliency

1. What strategies do you rely on when pressure or pain hits?

....

....

....

....

....

2. What does it feel like to stare down something intimidating—and keep going?

....

....

....

....

....

3. When overwhelmed, how do you anchor yourself so you don't freeze or quit?

....

....

....

....

....

4. What triggers irritation for you—and how do your internal reactions shape your response?

....

....

....

....

....

5. On a tough day, what's helped shift your mood or mindset for the better?

....

....

....

....

....

6. What do you do to reset or center—and how long does the benefit stick around?

....

....

....

....

....

7. When things go sideways, what inner dialogue do you notice most?

....

....

....

....

....

Connection and Engagement

1. What gesture from someone else made a lasting impression on you?

....

....

....

....

....

2. Who made you laugh recently—and what was it about the moment that stuck with you?

....

....

....

....

....

3. What would your ideal day with a friend or family member include?

....

....

....

....

....

4. What message of gratitude would you offer to someone who supported you lately?

....

....

....

....

....

5. What meaningful or curious questions could you ask to build connection with a new acquaintance?

....

....

....

....

....

6. What friend from the past would you catch up with—and what kind of conversation would unfold?

....

....

....

....

....

7. What kind of simple or meaningful date would help you feel present and engaged?

....

....

....

....

....

Healthy Living

1. How are you doing mentally, emotionally, and physically today? What's one thing that could help you feel a bit stronger in any of those areas?

....

....

....

....

....

2. Do you feel more at ease on sunny days or cloudy ones? What makes that setting feel right to you?

....

....

....

....

....

3. Which foods help you feel sharper, stronger, or more grounded?

....

....

....

....

....

4. What would make your bedroom feel like a calm, restful space —and help you recharge better?

....

....

....

....

....

5. What training setup would you love at home—and how would it help you stay active and strong?

....

....

....

....

....

6. If fear stepped aside, what bold or new experiences would you give yourself permission to try?

....

....

....

....

....

7. When your week goes smoothly, how do you feel—and how does that affect the way you show up in daily life?

....

....

....

....

....

Goals and Purpose

1. What fuels your drive when a goal feels tough? Why does that source of motivation stick with you?

....

....

....

....

....

2. When fear creeps in, what practical steps do you take to find clarity or calm?

....

....

....

....

....

3. Would you aim to ease depression or anxiety in the world—and what drives that choice?

....

....

....

....

....

4. What wins from your past show your resilience—and what fueled your progress?

....

....

....

....

....

5. If one meaningful goal could be realized, what would it be—and how would it shape your life?

....

....

....

....

....

6. What's standing between you and that goal—and what strengths could help you bridge the gap?

....

....

....

....

....

7. If a friend hesitated at a challenge, how would you help him see his potential and courage?

....

....

....

....

....

Calm and Resiliency

1. What series do you never tire of—and what themes or moments resonate with you most?

....

....

....

....

....

2. When tension rises in certain situations, what strategy works best for staying grounded?

....

....

....

....

....

3. What stressed you out recently—and how would you adjust your response next time around?

....

....

....

....

....

4. Pen a note to your stress explaining how you've found steadier ground and won't be shaken so easily.

....

....

....

....

....

5. What difficult moment hit hardest lately—and how did you find your way back to center?

....

....

....

....

....

6. What would your ideal workspace look like—and how would it help you stay focused without feeling stressed?

....

....

....

....

....

7. What tracks fire you up and fuel your confidence? What makes them powerful to you?

....

....

....

....

....

Connection and Engagement

1. What five interests or values do you think your best friends hold dear—and would they agree?

....

....

....

....

....

2. If generosity were the goal, where would you shop—and what meaningful item would you pick?

....

....

....

....

....

3. If you had a day stuck in transit with a public figure, who would it be—and what wisdom or stories would you explore?

....

....

....

....

....

4. How do your trusted people show up for you—and what actions make the biggest impact?

....

....

....

....

....

5. What would be a fulfilling or relaxing way to spend time with someone you care about?

....

....

....

....

....

6. What message of accountability or regret would you offer if you had the chance?

....

....

....

....

....

7. What kind of day would help you bond with your neighborhood or team?

....

....

....

....

....

Healthy Living

1. What actions have helped you push through tough mental days?

....

....

....

....

....

2. Picture your perfect lunch—where are you, what are you eating, and who's with you?

....

....

....

....

....

3. What small changes could help you fuel your body better this week?

....

....

....

....

....

4. When you don't sleep well, what habits could help you get better rest?

....

....

....

....

....

5. What physical activities help you reset or feel your best?

....

....

....

....

....

6. If you had a superpower, how would you use it to help others—and yourself?

....

....

....

....

....

7. What strengths do you admire in your best self—and how could you start building them now?

....

....

....

....

....

Goals and Purpose

1. What's going well in your life today, even in small ways?

....

....

....

....

....

2. What challenges are you facing, and what strengths might help shift your view?

....

....

....

....

....

3. Visualize something that brings you peace or strength. What's the emotional impact?

_____

_____

_____

_____

_____

4. How can you bring more clarity and focus to your daily actions toward your goals?

_____

_____

_____

_____

_____

5. What does a great day look like for you? What's one small step to help create it?

_____

_____

_____

_____

_____

6. What are you working on within yourself—and what actions move you forward?

....

....

....

....

....

7. What habits or actions help you break up the day and make parts of your routine feel more meaningful?

....

....

....

....

....

Calm and Resiliency

1. What places in your city offer you peace or a break from the noise?

....

....

....

....

....

2. What area of your home helps you unwind—and how could you use it better?

....

....

....

....

....

3. What personal item stands out as valuable to you—and why does it matter?

....

....

....

....

....

4. Breathe deeply—what image or action comes to mind that grounds you?

....

....

....

....

....

5. What do your friends notice about you when you're truly content?

....

....

....

....

....

6. Which colors in your wardrobe reflect your strength or tenacity?

_____

_____

_____

_____

_____

7. How did you feel after you let yourself cry? Did anything shift or make more sense afterward?

_____

_____

_____

_____

_____

Connection and Engagement

1. Who are the two people you lean on most? What about them builds your trust or respect?

....

....

....

....

....

2. Who's your go-to when life gets heavy? What do they say or do that really helps?

....

....

....

....

....

3. What team or social activities help you feel more steady or supported when stress kicks in?

....

....

....

....

....

4. What adventures or hangouts would you enjoy with a friend this month?

....

....

....

....

....

5. What goal would be meaningful to achieve with someone you respect? What's the first move?

....

....

....

....

....

6. Who are the key people in your life—and what's one way you can show them they matter?

....

....

....

....

....

7. Who's been on your mind lately? What message would you send to reconnect or check in?

....

....

....

....

....

Healthy Living

1. How well are you sleeping these days—and what's one change that might help you sleep better?

....

....

....

....

....

2. If one responsibility could disappear today, what would it be— and how would that help?

....

....

....

....

....

3. How do different kinds of weather—sun, wind, rain, or cold—affect your mood?

....

....

....

....

....

4. What's one skill or hobby you've been meaning to try? What might make it rewarding?

....

....

....

....

....

5. What concern is lingering for you—and what's a practical or calming first step to manage it?

....

....

....

....

....

6. Which day of the week feels best to you—and what routines make it feel that way?

....

....

....

....

....

7. What activity fits this kind of day—and why does it work well for your mood or energy?

....

....

....

....

....

Goals and Purpose

1. What's one practical goal you'd like to knock out this week?

....

....

....

....

....

2. What thought or mantra could keep you steady this week? How can you use it more intentionally?

....

....

....

....

....

3. Where in your life would you like more control—and how might that shift things for the better?

....

....

....

....

....

4. If you had a one-on-one with a leader you respect, what would you want to learn or share?

....

....

....

....

....

5. What's something in your community or daily environment you'd like to improve—and what's one way to start?

....

....

....

....

....

6. What's one way to strengthen your bonds this week—with friends, family, or partner?

....

....

....

....

....

7. What on your horizon is giving you energy or motivation right now?

....

....

....

....

....

Healthy Living

1. What do you do to keep your focus grounded in today rather than worrying about tomorrow?

....

....

....

....

....

2. What tools or practices help you take the pressure off when you're feeling tense?

....

....

....

....

....

3. How have you handled high-stress moments or panic before? What worked to get you through?

....

....

....

....

....

4. What challenge tested your limits and built your resilience?

....

....

....

....

....

5. Is there an outfit that feels like armor or comfort for you— what's the story behind it?

....

....

....

....

....

6. How can you be a calming presence for someone else today—even in small ways?

....

....

....

....

....

7. What positive moment from this week stands out—and why did it mean something to you?

....

....

....

....

....

Connection and Engagement

1. Who haven't you caught up with in a while—and how would you break the ice when you do?

....

....

....

....

....

2. Who in your circle gives you a sense of emotional safety? What traits make them feel reliable?

....

....

....

....

....

3. What did you and your best friend talk about last? How did the exchange make you feel?

....

....

....

....

....

4. What kind of teamwork or bonding moments help you reset emotionally?

....

....

....

....

....

5. Are you more energized by playful friends or those with calm energy? Why?

....

....

....

....

....

6. What meaningful gift have you received—and what thoughtful gesture have you made for someone else?

....

....

....

....

....

7. Think back to a hilarious moment shared with a buddy—what made it unforgettable?

....

....

....

....

....

Healthy Living

1. What five habits help you stay mentally sharp and balanced?

....

....

....

....

....

2. When did you last feel overwhelmed? What were the main stressors?

....

....

....

....

....

3. What's something you've done recently that energized you?

....

....

....

....

....

4. What routines from last year supported your well-being? Are they still part of your life?

....

....

....

....

....

5. Who pushes you to be better? What would a day together look like?

....

....

....

....

....

6. How do you stay on track with wellness when emotions run high?

....

....

....

....

....

7. What mental barriers hinder your health progress?

....

....

....

....

....

Goals and Purpose

1. What tweak can you make now to set the week up for success?

....

....

....

....

....

2. What self-talk keeps you grounded when plans derail?

....

....

....

....

....

3. What's your top priority goal at this moment?

....

....

....

....

....

4. Picture your life two years ahead—what's happening?

....

....

....

....

....

5. What advice would you share with someone aiming high?

....

....

....

....

....

6. What tweaks can enhance your morning or evening rituals?

....

....

....

....

....

7. What objective next week would give you a sense of achievement?

....

....

....

....

....

Calm and Resiliency

1. How do you steady yourself when things feel too much?

....

....

....

....

....

2. What should you pass on this week to stay focused?

....

....

....

....

....

3. How can you adjust your space to feel more relax?

....

....

....

....

....

4. What situations unsettle you, and how do you manage them?

....

....

....

....

....

5. How would you spend a cost-free afternoon to recharge?

....

....

....

....

....

Calm and Resiliency

6. Acknowledge your strength in overcoming challenges.

....

....

....

....

....

7. What accomplishments this week made you feel capable?

....

....

....

....

....

Connection and Engagement

1. How can you strengthen your inner dialogue?

....

....

....

....

....

2. What communication habits can improve your relationships?

....

....

....

....

....

3. What gestures can show appreciation to those you care about?

....

....

....

....

....

4. How can you be of service to those around you?

....

....

....

....

....

5. What group activities energize you and your friends?

....

....

....

....

....

6. What actions can strengthen your role as a friend?

....

....

....

....

....

7. Which self-care routines can become group activities?

....

....

....

....

....

Healthy Living

1. What limits do you set to keep yourself grounded during a demanding week?

....

....

....

....

....

2. What's your strategy for staying balanced around draining personalities?

....

....

....

....

....

3. When were you at your physical and emotional best? What did your routine look like then?

....

....

....

....

....

4. What would a full day of meals look like if your goal was steady energy and strength?

....

....

....

....

....

5. Which routines support you physically and mentally at the same time?

....

....

....

....

....

6. How do you stay focused and positive despite distractions or discouragement?

_____

_____

_____

_____

_____

7. What positive habits can replace alcohol or tobacco when you're feeling stressed?

_____

_____

_____

_____

_____

Goals and Purpose

1. How do you define a meaningful life for yourself?

....

....

....

....

....

2. What pivotal events have influenced the values you live by today?

....

....

....

....

....

3. What would feel like a productive and satisfying win for you this weekend?

....

....

....

....

....

4. What's one recent success you're genuinely proud of?

....

....

....

....

....

5. What win from this week made you feel capable and steady?

....

....

....

....

....

6. What's your top priority this month, and what makes it
important?

....

....

....

....

....

7. What action steps will help you stay focused and on track with
your goal?

....

....

....

....

....

Calm and Resiliency

1. Where have you felt most grounded and relaxed? What made it special?

....

....

....

....

....

2. What nighttime rituals help you recharge for tomorrow?

....

....

....

....

....

3. What's a dream that made you wake up with clarity or hope?

....

....

....

....

....

4. When did you last feel truly content? What were you doing?

....

....

....

....

....

5. What tools helped you reset after a recent challenge?

....

....

....

....

....

6. What music grounds you or helps you focus when you need it most?

....

....

....

....

....

7. What life lesson taught you to keep showing up, even when it's hard?

....

....

....

....

....

Connection and Engagement

1. What effort could you make to deepen trust or connection with someone important to you?

....

....

....

....

....

2. Is there someone you've held a grudge against? How might you begin letting go?

....

....

....

....

....

3. What's holding you back from releasing resentment? What firm boundary could support your peace?

....

....

....

....

....

4. Who do you look up to, and what traits do they model that you respect?

....

....

....

....

....

5. Who stands out as a steady, positive force in your life—and what have they done to earn that place?

....

....

....

....

....

6. What's a simple yet sincere way you could show appreciation to those who support you?

....

....

....

....

....

7. What cause aligns with your values? How could you take action, even in a small way?

....

....

....

....

....

Healthy Living

1. What are five tasks stressing you out right now? What's your game plan for managing each one?

....

....

....

....

....

2. What role does mental strength or clarity play in how you handle challenges?

....

....

....

....

....

3. What's your mental state like today? What would help you feel more centered or steady?

....

....

....

....

....

4. If you could talk freely to someone about your mental health, what would you want them to understand?

....

....

....

....

....

5. If a friend asked you whether therapy helps, what would you tell them from your perspective?

....

....

....

....

....

6. Which emotions are front and center for you today? What's driving them?

....

....

....

....

....

7. Jot a quick message to yourself about the importance of staying emotionally strong and balanced.

....

....

....

....

....

Goals and Purpose

1. Looking back three years, how has your life or mindset evolved? What sparked that growth?

....

....

....

....

....

2. What saying or quote do you live by when life throws you a curveball?

....

....

....

....

....

3. How do you handle setbacks when you're pushing toward something important?

....

....

....

....

....

4. What personal lesson stood out most to you this year about what drives your choices?

....

....

....

....

....

5. What book or film is calling your name lately—and what are you hoping it offers?

....

....

....

....

....

6. What's one project or goal you've been putting off that you could knock out this weekend?

....

....

....

....

....

7. If you gave your time to a cause, what would align with your values and strengths?

....

....

....

....

....

Calm and Resiliency

1. Is there a belief that's been holding you back? What's a practical way to challenge or let it go?

....

....

....

....

....

2. Recall a moment of anxiety. What signs did you notice? What would you do differently today?

....

....

....

....

....

3. What do you think someone who truly knows you would say to counter your anxious thoughts?

....

....

....

....

....

4. What's your experience with breathwork? How does a deep breath impact your calm or focus?

....

....

....

....

....

5. What's a fear you're working on releasing? How have you tried facing it or reducing its power?

....

....

....

....

....

6. How likely are your fears to come true? What evidence challenges or supports them?

....

....

....

....

....

7. What tools or habits help you reset when anxiety shows up—either ones you use or are curious about?

....

....

....

....

....

Connection and Engagement

1. What practical steps could strengthen your bond with those closest to you?

....

....

....

....

....

2. Where do you need firmer lines to protect your energy and peace of mind?

....

....

....

....

....

3. Are you able to stand your ground when guilt is used against you? What would help you say no with strength?

....

....

....

....

....

4. How do you uplift others when you're together? What impact do you want to have?

....

....

....

....

....

5. What mental prep or tools help you navigate hard conversations without letting anxiety take over?

....

....

....

....

....

6. Is there a character whose confidence or integrity you respect? How could you embody that more?

....

....

....

....

....

7. What shared experiences could help you reconnect and make new memories?

....

....

....

....

....

Healthy Living

1. What roadblocks did you hit while trying to stay healthy—mentally or physically?

....

....

....

....

....

2. What actions, habits, or mindset shifts helped you push through the tough spots?

....

....

....

....

....

3. How would you describe your current mental and emotional state? Where are you steady, and where is there tension?

....

....

....

....

....

4. What new or continued health practices do you want to bring into the next year?

....

....

....

....

....

5. Has journaling offered you structure, insight, or calm? How so?

....

....

....

....

....

6. Which physical activities feel like a good fit for your lifestyle and goals?

_____

_____

_____

_____

_____

7. How can you build resilience so future stress doesn't knock you off course?

_____

_____

_____

_____

_____

Goals and Purpose

1. What recent accomplishment gave you a sense of pride? What effort or resilience made it happen?

....

....

....

....

....

2. What goal would excite you most to accomplish in the coming year?

....

....

....

....

....

3. What's a realistic plan or habit you can build to get momentum on a current goal?

....

....

....

....

....

4. What personal shifts—mental, emotional, or behavioral—have stood out since you started?

....

....

....

....

....

5. What truths or mantras can guide your mindset as you move forward?

....

....

....

....

....

6. What five milestones, changes, or insights have defined your journaling year?

....

....

....

....

....

7. Honor your consistency and growth—write yourself a message that recognizes your effort.

....

....

....

....

....

Keep Growing, Keep Asking:
Discover More Titles

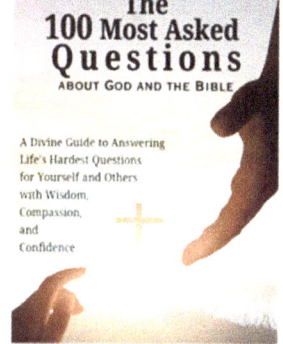

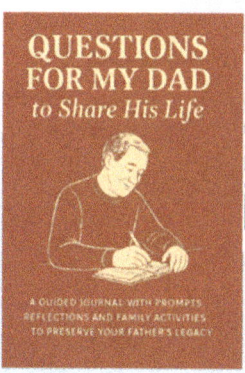

www.ingramcontent.com/pod-product-compliance
Lightning Source LLC
Chambersburg PA
CBHW071147120626
46546CB00006B/2155